HEALING
self care for leaders and their teams

ANNA ELIATAMBY
WITH GRAZIA LOMONTE

Copyright © 2024 Healthy Leadership CIC

The moral right of the author has been asserted.

Apart from any fair dealing for the purposes of research or private study, or criticism or review, as permitted under the Copyright, Designs and Patents Act 1988, this publication may only be reproduced, stored, or transmitted, in any form or by any means, with the prior permission in writing of the publishers, or in the case of reprographic reproduction in accordance with the terms of licenses issued by the Copyright Licensing Agency.

Enquiries concerning reproduction outside those
terms should be sent to the publishers.

ISBN: 978-1-80443-065-1 (Paperback)
ISBN: 978-1-80443-066-8 (Ebook)

British Library Cataloguing in Publication Data.
A catalogue record for this book is available from the British Library.

CONTENTS

Acknowledgements v
Introduction vii
Getting Ready to Explore xi

SECTION 1: LEARNING ABOUT YOUR QUALITIES AND BEHAVIOURS..1

1. Leadership Qualities and Behaviours............................3
2. Managing Stress, Well-Being, and Coping 14
3. Cherishing and Refining My Leadership 29

SECTION 2: LEARNING ABOUT AND LIVING WITH THE UNDERLYING AND UNRESOLVED 39

Introduction 41
Above And Below The Surface 44
Rebuilding Your Frame of Reference 52

SECTION 3: WELL-BEING FOR YOUR TEAM 75

Introduction 77
Factors That Impact Well-Being 80

References 93

ACKNOWLEDGEMENTS

We owe a debt of gratitude to many people, colleagues, family, and friends.

Greg Parston, who shares his own story, is a vibrant guide and mentor. He was and is instrumental in leading and introducing many global and national initiatives for a better life for many. Greg's support and guidance have shaped Anna's thinking, creativity, and career. He has guided those of us who are lucky to know Greg to do our best for the greater good.

Ambassador William Lacy Swing, former Director General of IOM (UN Migration Agency), was an exceptional and consummate leader. He gently guided all of us who were privileged to work with him. He naturally encouraged us to work with dignity and respect for the people we served. He was a man of integrity, without exception.

Brittany White was extremely helpful in gathering research on stress and well-being. She is very creative and skilled. Thanks to Alison Smith of Blue Daze Designs for the artwork and to Robin Philips (Shilka Publishing) for his help and support.

And, to all our teachers, guides, and mentors: thank you.

INTRODUCTION

Our ambition propels us into leadership. We adopt and assume key characteristics and behaviours to lead. Some of these choices are based on our history, personality, and experience of other people's leadership.

Our leadership behaviours and personality are, we assume, fully formed and functional. But we often forget to look after ourselves as we power through our trailblazer roles. We focus on the helpful parts of our personality and ignore the unresolved aspects that can hold us back. We forget to give ourselves space and time to appreciate our personality and resolve the often-ignored parts of ourselves, and, therefore, heal.

For us to grow and flourish as leaders so that we lead inclusively and healthily, we need to pause and look at our own well-being and self-care. Unmanaged stress, both temporary and long-term, can have a harmful impact on our ability to function and lead. And there are so many pressures and uncertainties for leaders and others in the world today.

It is vital that we look after our own mental health and well-being. This will free us to be the best leader we can be.

When we take care of ourselves and ensure the same for our staff and teams, we experience increased productivity, higher morale, and well-being. Some of this can depend on how much personnel think we are looking after ourselves and how well we lead. People are more likely to look after themselves at work if they see leaders manage their self-care and lead healthily without resorting to toxicity.

Focussing on internal and intrinsic factors as individuals, leaders, and team members has a greater impact on well-being than concentrating on external factors. Internal factors include personal growth and relationships, and extrinsic ones comprise fame and wealth, etc.

Our book is based on our definition of healthy leadership and healthy organisations where everybody strives for decency. Healthiness is an essential ingredient for decency. Without it, we are likely to be unsuccessful.

The words "healthy" and "healthiness" refer to physical and, sometimes, mental health and well-being. These facets are important components for overall healthiness, and we suggest that there are others. These include synergy between purpose, values, and how we live and work; the impact of material resources and the environment; being willing to be open and listen to the incoming future; and how we live and cope with the shadow side.

To promote overall health, we need to coordinate these factors with compassion and respect. Collective responsibility for promoting the helpful and addressing the unhelpful should be present.

The term "golden" represents helpful qualities like kindness, integrity, compassion, and purposeful work. The shadow includes dishonesty, bullying, and harassment. They are interlinked and can reflect each other's opposites.

Leadership is an individual and collective function that has many intentions. This includes an aim to serve human beings and/or something else. Some people operationalize leadership ethically and positively to serve others. Others will have another focus, such as a profit motive, alongside wanting to be ethical.

Healthy leadership involves serving others ethically and respectfully, even in the face of negativity. A healthy leader remains flexible and open to sensing the incoming future. Being and growing as a healthy leader ensures decency in yourself and in how you act at work.

HEALTHY ORGANISATIONS

Why do organisations exist? To serve a greater purpose, which is sometimes forgotten as the organisation becomes bigger and veers from the intended path.

A healthy organisation ensures it remains true to its purpose and does no harm to humans or the planet. Do no harm. The organisation strives to create a nurturing environment for people to grow and succeed in their work. A healthy organisation recognizes and addresses unhealthy aspects, embraces change, and plans for the future while working in the present.

Decency is a core essential and its use flows naturally throughout the organisation. People do not have to think about the need to be decent, they just are. Thus, the organisation contributes to the greater decency we need for the world.

We use our perspective of healthy leadership to help you explore, firstly, your own behaviours, stress management, and well-being.

Secondly, we help you investigate the unknown and unresolved parts of yourself.

Thirdly, we assist you and your team to explore both the cherished and unresolved aspects.

In each section, there are reflections and activities to enable your self-exploration. The choice is yours in terms of how much you want to investigate. We all choose different paths when we pause and reflect. Our ideas are based on the Decency Journey pocketbooks and associated Linkedin articles.

Let's start.

GETTING READY TO EXPLORE

Welcome. Thanks for selecting this book. We hope you will take time to read and explore your wonderful qualities as a leader and as a member of our society.

It is possible that you are already feeling stressed. It may be too difficult to make time to carry out the reflections that we have described below. Here are a few suggestions that may help you in the short term.

Please start by pressing pause in your life. Cherish who you are and what you have achieved as a leader. Praise yourself. Perhaps give yourself a gift.

Then look around and see where you can slot in 30 minutes to rest and relax. Ideally, this should be a daily practice. Secondly, just focus on your breathing and relearn deep breathing.

Thirdly, consider your self-care when you looked after yourself better. Reintroduce one or two habits to enhance your current approach.

Please ensure that you do the above. Once you have stabilised, then please plan to read the book and carry out the reflections.

How did I become a leader?

I am a democratic leader. At least, that is the style I have created and live by. It feels natural to me, but there are other styles that lurk. Some of these can be useful, such as being autocratic in an emergency. I know my approaches and their impact. If I am feeling benevolent and self-assured, then I will be democratic. If, however, I am stressed or threatened, then my default is to be autocratic. And, on the rare occasion, downright bombastic.

Fortunately, I am rarely autocratic. And when I am, I self-correct, mostly. And I apologise when needed. So where do these styles come from?

There is an expectation, in my family, of excelling, of leading, and of living by values through democracy. I was not explicitly aware of this in my early days. Then I met some of my relatives and learned about my father and what he lived for. My maternal grandfather, Nathaniel Ramachandra, was ethical and a democratic leader, but quiet about how he lived and worked. My paternal great-grandfather, Reverend Samuel Eliatamby, was a pastor in Uduvil in north Sri Lanka. He died in 1921, but people still remember him for his work and how he lived. (There were other relatives who did almost the exact opposite of being value-based. They taught me about what not to do and be.)

So why did I notice and adopt the helpful? The influencing force was my value base, despite my intense ambition, which I did not recognise in my early days, and my self-esteem and respect for myself. And perhaps, wanting to be like the more ethical people in my life, such as my father.

At school, in my studies, and at work, I saw and experienced many leaders, styles, and behaviours. From the best to the manipulative to the worst.

The resolved and unresolved parts of my personality influence some of my leadership style. I have autistic qualities, so being democratic enables me to have space as I permit staff to grow and carry out responsibilities in their own way. I also need to build in "Anna time" so that I can retreat into my introversion to rebalance.

Why am I autocratic sometimes? Perhaps because I feel that this style could be useful, especially when I want to control not lead? My autocratic behaviour stems from unresolved issues in my past.

That is my story. All of us, as leaders, have a similar story to tell and learn from. For us to grow and develop, we need to explore our story and build from it so we can heal.

We also need to learn how to look after our personal mental health and well-being. And that is a rare thing for a leader to do.

As people say, if we don't look after ourselves, we can't look after others. And the latter is part of our duty of care and responsibility. Let's start the self-analysis.

SECTION ONE

LEARNING ABOUT YOUR QUALITIES AND BEHAVIOURS

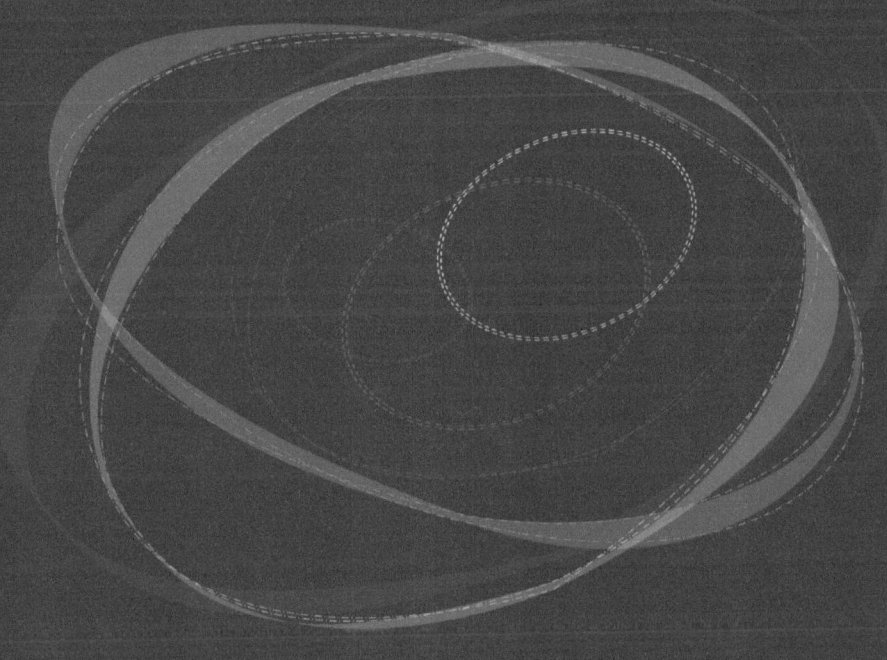

There are three chapters:

1. An exploration to help you identify your leadership qualities and behaviours.

2. Understanding your response to stress and pressure. Learning about your self-care strategies.

3. Cherishing and building your leadership qualities and behaviours.

CHAPTER 1

LEADERSHIP QUALITIES AND BEHAVIOURS

I have always been impatient – since I was a boy – and one downside of that, I know, can be a lack of attention, including to oneself. Concern for personal self-care and well-being can seem selfish as you push to get stuff done.

Perhaps the thing that most changed that neglect for me was a directive from my boss, early in my career, to "make time".

I was a young vice president in a New York City medical centre back in 1981. My job was to put together a strategy for a "medical school without walls", which entailed working collaboratively with academic associates and clinical partners to distribute healthcare responsibilities in centres of excellence across the borough of Brooklyn. The aim was to focus the collective provision explicitly on improving the health of our community and not just on attaining academic or institutional success. I was very busy.

As part of the executive team, I often met with the president – a clinical specialist turned chief executive – to discuss our strategy, to try to solve what were often associated political problems, and to seize opportunities that had emerged. Sometimes my boss used those meetings to consider critically – as good management demands – my performance in these realms, not just in an "annual review" but as part of the everyday.

In one such assessment meeting, the president asked me when I reflected on my work. I was a little surprised by the question, almost wanting to say: "I don't have time for that sort of junk", when he also asked to see my calendar. Of course, it was chock-full of scheduled meetings, day by day, hour by hour.

The president scanned the pages, looked up and said: "I want you to wipe Thursday mornings free." When I questioned why he was erasing 10% of my available work week, he said to me: "When do you make time to think? To ask yourself if we're doing the right stuff? To question yourself and what we're achieving?" I certainly didn't put much emphasis on any of that "soft stuff" at the time but, with his instruction, he was insisting that I make time to do just that.

I went back to my office and obediently asked my assistant to "wipe Thursday mornings free". That first free morning was a little weird for me. I recall sitting alone in my office, asking myself, rather awkwardly, questions about me and my work, and my team. But the questions raised some uncomfortable answers and some challenges to my impatient working. New thinking began to emerge.

This enforced self-reflection changed my work and my working relationships, as well as my self-awareness and my confidence. Indeed, my boss' simple directive changed my working life forever. For over time, freeing time simply "to think" became a weekly practice – usually on a Thursday morning – that I lived with for the next three decades.

On one of those first free mornings, the president had also arranged for me to see a "coach", whom he had worked with during his earlier academic days in Massachusetts. Not just any coach, I was soon to appreciate, but the inimitable Richard Beckhard, one of the founders of organisational development, who – over the next 18 years – was to become my coach and mentor, especially after I moved to London and formed my own social enterprise. Dick questioned, pushed, criticised, and supported me in manners, which strengthened my purpose and resolve.

I have learned from all of that. Making time to think, exposing myself – sometimes with the help of a "disinterested" outsider – to often sceptical questions and critique, and consciously reflecting on why and what I

> do are as central to my personal well-being as keeping physically fit and healthy.
>
> I would suggest too that this "critical self-thinking" is particularly important for those of us whose work and purpose is to improve the social results of others. That is because our bottom lines are messy and conflictive and are not measurable simply by a unifying financial outcome. And that's because, on reflection, you learn from that messiness and from those conflicts that you simply don't know – you don't know what the people on whose "result" you are focused really need and want (and what the difference is), or what your partners are truly driven by or what you can do, cannot do, and need help to do.
>
> You don't know until you make time to think.
>
> Greg Parston, co-founder and former CE of the Office for Public Management

As Greg said, self-reflection is not an easy skill to develop; neither is knowing what type of leader we want to be. There are many lists and sets of leadership competences that we could look at, analyse, and then include. If you look through most of them, they focus on the fit to the responsibility and the job, not the personal qualities and associated behaviours of a leader. And they concentrate on the helpful and aspirational, not the less desired and, sometimes, often used.

Here is our list based on what we know of leadership. It moves beyond the traditional competences to include the human in all of us as leaders. The qualities reflect our day-to-day and deeper human needs – for ourselves and all humanity. And they acknowledge our frailties.

PERSONAL ASSETS

Sacrifice and simplicity: being willing to sacrifice yourself for the greater good, regardless of the organisation's purpose.

Integrity, kindness, and concern for others: having these at the centre of your core.

Peace for yourself and others: seeking harmony and reconciliation instead of competitiveness and unadulterated ambition.

For people: always putting others before yourself. We are part of a greater humanity, and our prime responsibility should be towards fellow citizens and their needs. Our needs and ambitions as leaders should be secondary.

Looking after personal mental health, physical health, and well-being: ensuring that you practise proper selfishness. Being able to cope with pressure and stress.

Accepting and recognising the role and influence of the past and present (resolved and unresolved): being willing to be on a journey of discovery, reflection, and pause. Growing and changing.

Even if our history has not been traumatic, we each have unresolved matters that may pop through into our current life and influence us. For example, reacting in a domineering and defensive manner to another leader because they remind you of someone who bullied you in the past. These are the hidden volcanoes of our lives. Some of these are active and others are almost permanently dormant. We will explore this more in the next section of the book.

WORK QUALITIES

Understanding, fairness, and equanimity: using fairness and equanimity to understand the situation and then decide on the best action. Promoting collective responsibility where the positive is praised, and toxicity is addressed openly.

Living values and purpose: knowing these and sticking to them regardless of the provocation. This includes personal and spiritual beliefs that guide you.

Admitting fault with humility: being willing to self-correct if needed.

Knowing how to communicate and interact: being person-centred and speaking with rather than at. Appreciating personal and cultural differences.

Understanding complexity: when faced with the complex: it is important to be open to confusion and to collaborate with others in examining the many facets of each situation. Pause and then act.

Knowing the difference between leadership and governance: appreciating your role as a leader and that of others. Being flexible but also sticking to agreed boundaries.

Dealing with crises: knowing how to understand the situation and remain fluid. Providing clarity in role and responsibility allocation. Listen, pause, and then act.

Thinking strategically: knowing how to lift yourself above the daily and prosaic to the higher ground of strategy without resorting to unnecessary jargon. Appreciating the difference between operation and strategy.

Creating a work environment that facilitates well-being: working with staff to create clear expectations in terms of behaviours. Developing a culture that promotes and maintains psychological health.

Treating others with dignity and respect: regardless of that person's seniority.

Paying attention to community and world responsibilities: understanding your place in the world and working to leave a legacy for future generations.

SELF-ANALYSIS: LEADERSHIP QUALITIES

Stop and think about your leadership. Pause and remember a few seminal moments where you could celebrate your style and qualities. And times when you came unstuck or that you have regretted. Reflect on these as you go through the table below so you can unpack your qualities.

My moments

Quality	The behaviours I use	How did I learn them?	What is their usual impact?
Personal assets			
Sacrifice and simplicity			
Integrity, kindness, and concern for others			
Peace for yourself and others			
For people			
Looking after personal mental health, physical health, and well-being			

Accepting and recognising the role and influence of the past and present (resolved and unresolved)			
Work qualities			
Understanding, fairness, and equanimity			
Living values and purpose			
Admitting fault with humility			
Knowing how to communicate and interact			
Understanding complexity			
Knowing the difference between leadership and governance			
Dealing with crises			

Thinking strategically			
Creating a work environment that facilitates well-being			
Treating others with dignity and respect			
Paying attention to community and world responsibilities			

Having completed this, now think about what you know about your leadership behaviours and qualities. What leadership behaviours and qualities are easily recognizable, such as being kind? Which ones show that there are some underlying unresolved factors and that there is still work to be done, e.g., a tendency to be envious?

Known

Unknown

Based on the above, how would you describe your leadership style?

My leadership style is:

To what extent does this match how others see you?

CHAPTER 2

MANAGING STRESS, WELL-BEING, AND COPING

Now that you understand your leadership qualities, let's explore what maintains and affects you as a leader.

In this chapter, we will focus on pressures, stress management, well-being, and coping.

We'll provide you with reflections and questions to explore how these things affect your work and personal life.

Let's start by discussing the core concepts.

UNDERSTANDING THE CONCEPTS

What is stress?

The World Health Organization (2023) defines stress as "a state of worry or mental tension caused by a difficult situation" (World Health Organization, 2023). Often, stress can cause the release of hormones that allow you to deal with pressure and threats, also known as the "fight or flight" response. When you're only experiencing stress for a short period, those hormone levels will return to normal. If you're constantly under pressure or stressed, your hormone levels won't go back to normal, and you'll start showing stress symptoms.

Remember there is an optimal level of stress that is beneficial, and that we need. In this chapter, we focus on those occasions when stress is too much.

PRESSURES

These are internal and external factors that can lead to stress. Here is a depiction of the key areas in which pressures and triggers for stress could occur. They all interact with each other, both externally and within the person. Each area has general and specific helpful and unhelpful aspects. Some become pressure points for stress unhelpfully, and others act as motivators positively.

Each person has their own set of pressures. It is worth knowing about them and working out your reactions to each stressor. Here is a table showing commonly occurring pressures.

Home	Work	Health	Environment
Spouse	Manager	Nutrition	Security
Children	Role	Body weight	Transport
Finances	Communication	Lack of exercise	Noise
In-laws	Direct reports	Lack of rest	Traffic
Time management	Peers	Poor work-life balance	Temperature
Illness in the family	Toxic cultures – bullying, harassment, discrimination	Caffeine	Technology
Pets	Lack of recognition	Impact of weathering	Crowding
Home maintenance	Job security	Aging	Pollution
Friends	Office space	Physical health	Global warming
Work / life boundaries	Workload and deadlines	Mental health	Economy
	Policy directives	Food and drink	Cultural differences

How we cope with each pressure is an indicator of how we manage stress. If we think we can control each pressure or just need to accept each one, then we are unlikely to be managing stress well. If we believe we can influence or manage stress, we are likely handling it well.

STRESS REACTIONS AND SIGNS

There are three types of stress reaction: cognitive, emotional, and physical. (And there is often an overlap between stress reactions and signs.)

Cognitive reactions include an impact on memory. Stress and worry take up space in your short-term memory, making it harder to remember things, recall, etc.

There can also be a negative impact on attention. You can, for a moment, lose your ability to concentrate, or focus on the wrong detail or spread your attention too widely.

You may pay too much attention to your biases and preferences, and this can skew your thinking.

Your decision-making may be out of balance. Usually, we maintain a synergy between emotions and logic to make decisions. If we are unduly stressed, then we can decide from an imbalance – too much emotion or too much logic.

Emotional reactions include suppression or being volatile. Or just being out of control with your emotions. Your breathing is likely to be negatively affected and you could be shallow breathing or holding your breath, or only taking a breath when necessary. It is important to know and understand all your stress reactions.

Reactions and responses will vary depending on your mindset/role and what else is going in your life. If you have many pressures and you doubt yourself, the chances are that you will not be managing your stress. If you have a positive mindset and many pressures, you are likely to cope.

Signs can include physical and mental symptoms like aches, chest pain, exhaustion, trouble sleeping, headaches, high blood pressure, muscle tension, digestive issues, weakened immune system, anxiety, depression, panic attacks, and sadness. Chronic stress "can worsen pre-existing health problems… [and] can also cause or exacerbate mental health conditions, most commonly anxiety and depression" (World Health Organization, 2023).

Stress can make it hard to relax, cause anxiety, irritability, and difficulty concentrating. It can also lead to headaches, body pains, upset stomach, and trouble sleeping. It can also result in other dietary effects, such as a loss of appetite or an increase in eating habits.

People dealing with chronic stress may resort to unhealthy behaviours such as excessive drinking, gambling, or drug use. ("Stress: signs, symptoms, management, & prevention", 2021).

Being stressed can also negatively affect your leadership style and behaviours, especially if you do not manage it. Someone may choose to use an ineffective leadership style, not think clearly, and delegate inappropriately, etc. You could be emotionally volatile, ignore people's emotions, be pessimistic, and try to power through stress. You may not be alert to all the important incoming data, i.e., have poor situational awareness. If any of these factors are present, then staff are likely to lack energy and motivation. They may not be productive and happy and there could be increased conflict.

WHAT IS WELL-BEING?

Stress management and living a healthy lifestyle are linked to well-being. The Cambridge Dictionary (well-being, n.d.) defines well-being as "the state of feeling happy and healthy". Well-being encompasses various aspects including physical, emotional, social, psychological, and economic well-being and life satisfaction, development and activity, and engaging activities and work.

Well-being is often measured by researchers using questionnaires and objective data, such as income and employment. Well-being relies on good health, positive social relationships, and access to basic resources. The lack of these key components to well-being could cause an individual to suffer significant amounts of stress until the issue is resolved.

Wellness is considered "an important element of well-being" (Pendell, 2021) and includes "habits of eating, physical activity and quality sleep that lead to positive health outcomes".

WHAT WELLNESS ISN'T

In order to promote their products as healthy, "wellness" marketing agencies and businesses use scientific-sounding words. To back their claims, companies will often follow unproven health trends, such as "activated charcoal", to gain consumer trust (Raphael, 2023). To make their product appear scientific and healthy, some brands include vitamin C, even if it is in tiny amounts.

Brands can assert that research supports their product by creating websites with links to findings. They often claim that these studies back their product, but they are often data summaries that do not mention their product, do not support their claims, and are cherry-picked to imply an unproven correlation.

The wellness industry lacks proper regulation beyond one simple rule: not to lie outright. Some skirt this rule with clever wording and barely discernible disclaimers.

Since wellness has become an industry, it isn't interested in promoting wellness and health as efficiently as it could. In fact, the wellness industry "relies on widespread sections of the global population regarding themselves as unhealthy … diagnosing themselves as not up to scratch, and then spending to "try to fix it" (Hendy, 2023). To generate more revenue, businesses in this industry constantly find additional reasons to make their clients unhappy.

Consumers looking for stress relief may get caught up in the wellness industry and feel even more stressed trying to keep up with the latest trends.

Wellness means more than just following health trends on social media. It involves taking care of yourself through sleep, healthy eating, exercise, and self-awareness.

MENTAL HEALTH VERSUS MENTAL ILLNESS

There is a continuum between mental health and mental illness. We experience these to varying degrees, sometimes daily. Some of us will need specialist mental health support for times when life becomes overwhelming or just all the time. The rest of us will be healthy most times and may, on occasion, need time out or specialist support.

Regardless of the state of our mental health, we deserve respect and support. We are all citizens of the world, and very few of us are normal, if such a state exists. We need to understand ourselves and work out how best to maintain our mental health and well-being.

YOUR FRAME OF REFERENCE

Your mindset and associated role are your frame of reference through which you see yourself and then the world. They influence your sense of self, behaviours, actions, thoughts, and emotions. They comprise helpful and unhelpful elements.

Your frame of reference underpins your leadership character. Very good actors absorb their character and move into the role. They show the mindset and role by what they say, their actions, and emotions. We do the same, sometimes inadvertently.

A frame of reference will help you cope and have a good amount of self-respect. A mixed mindset/role of positives and the unresolved can also be useful if you function from your helpful core.

We all have various mindsets and roles. It is, therefore, important to understand your mindsets and roles. Appreciating how your past, present, and future influence and shape these mindsets and roles is crucial.

WHAT IS HEALING?

When we think of a physical injury or wound, we talk about healing. To do so, we need a salve, perhaps medication, and support. We hope to have our bodies return to what they used to be, perhaps with a scar or two.

We don't use the same approach for psychological injuries or wounds unless we are already accessing mental health support. Most of us have a range of small and large psychological injuries and wounds that we usually ignore or find ways of healing from them. These are always in the background and can interfere with our daily lives.

Healing psychologically involves accepting and reflecting on your injuries and wounds to live a more balanced life.

And you must, of necessity, be prepared to look at your helpful and unhelpful approaches and reconcile both. This means that it will be necessary to investigate your past and present, the known and unknown, resolved, and unresolved. These are the volcanoes, dormant and active. However, it is always best to do this when you are in the right frame of mind – feeling calm and ready to explore.

COPING STRATEGIES AND HABITS

Our adult life is full of habits, and these are part of our role. Some of them help us regulate and manage our complicated lives. Some of these we will have built from the people in our history. Others we will have assimilated from TV, social media, and sometimes professionals paid to help us. Setting the alarm clock to start our morning routine. Creating a menu for the week and buying the ingredients. Habits we have with our partners that maintain the relationship. These contribute to our sense of self and the associated respect and esteem.

These are all coping habits and can be helpful and good for you or the opposite. There are many layers to them.

We use them to reinforce our mindset and role, which can vary from helpful to unhelpful, sometimes in a heartbeat. What we use can also depend on our circumstances. For example, if we are extremely stressed, doubt may arise, leading us to rely on unhelpful habits that reinforce that doubt.

We argue that there is an interaction between the coping strategies we use, our sense of self, and what is resolved and unresolved in our personal and work life. For instance, excelling in a global project, but then submitting a below par paper to the leadership the next day. It's almost like you must punish yourself for excelling. Because your self-esteem is not constant.

This diagram depicts the key areas in which we need coping habits.

FRAME OF REFERENCE

HEALTH AND WELL-BEING	RELATIONSHIPS (personal and work)
Self-care plan	Quality and quantity
The past	
Balance	
Mental health and physical health	
Beliefs and faith	

MINDSET
Self-respect,
Values/Purpose,
History

PRACTICAL MATTERS	LEADERSHIP QUALITIES
Finance	Personal assets
Place to live	Work qualities
Transport	
Recreation	

HEALTH AND WELL-BEING

We need to have a proactive self-care plan for the day to day and emergencies in both our personal and professional life. We must acknowledge our past and its role in our current life – be that helpful or unhelpful. Maintaining our mental health and physical health is essential, including times when we need specialist help or time away. And giving space for our beliefs and faith is important. All this will lead to a good sense of balance in our life, from work to personal and vice versa.

The self-care plan includes understanding our pressures and stress reactions, and creating healthy habits for physical actions, healthy living, and excellent support. Ensuring that we look after our practical matters should also be part of the self-care plan.

RELATIONSHIPS

We need to have, at least, one or two people in our life who will support us, regardless. They form the backbone of our support. Others, including partners, friends, and family, can help, as could colleagues.

What is important is the quality of the relationships, not just the quantity. Relationships are vital for our lives and well-being.

LEADERSHIP QUALITIES

It is not enough to have and develop these, but we must also maintain them using good coping strategies, such as having good work habits. Encouraging self-learning through reflection and mentorship and seeking feedback from junior employees is vital.

PRACTICAL MATTERS

Where we live, how we manage (or not) our finances impact our leadership and well-being. Transport and recreation also have a great impact. If any of these are not helpful, then they can negatively affect our ability to cope, e.g. an overly long commute to work.

CAVEAT

It is unlikely that, in each area, we will only have helpful coping habits and strategies. We are human and fallible. We need to name both the helpful and unhelpful in each quadrant. Then look at the extent to which our values and sense of self influence our coping habits.

Here are some examples of helpful and unhelpful coping strategies.

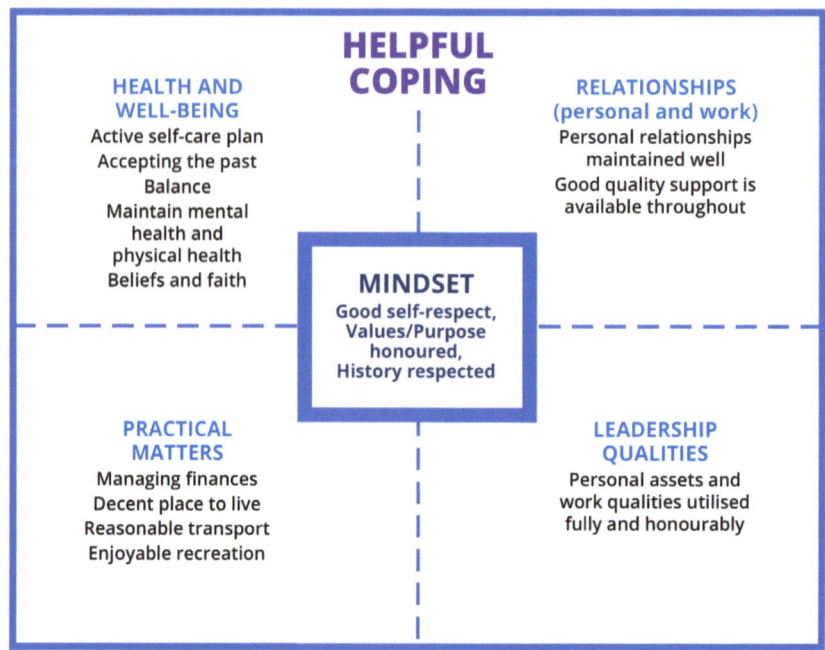
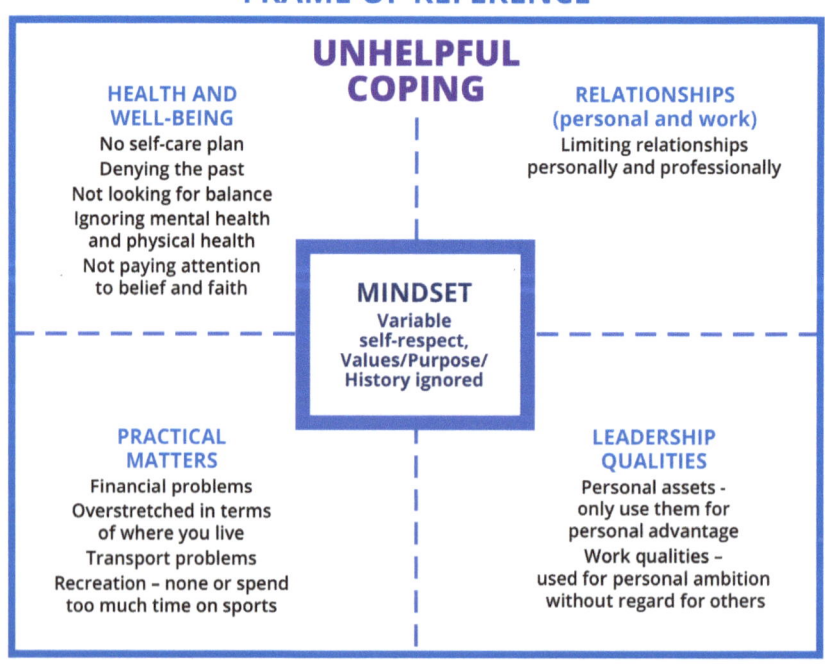

SELF-ANALYSIS PRESSURES, STRESS REACTIONS, AND COPING HABITS

Look at the diagram below. Identify areas causing pressure and stress and write your responses to each one. What are your assets in each area? How effective are your reactions?

Now, please take some time to think about your own – helpful and unhelpful – coping strategies in each quadrant.

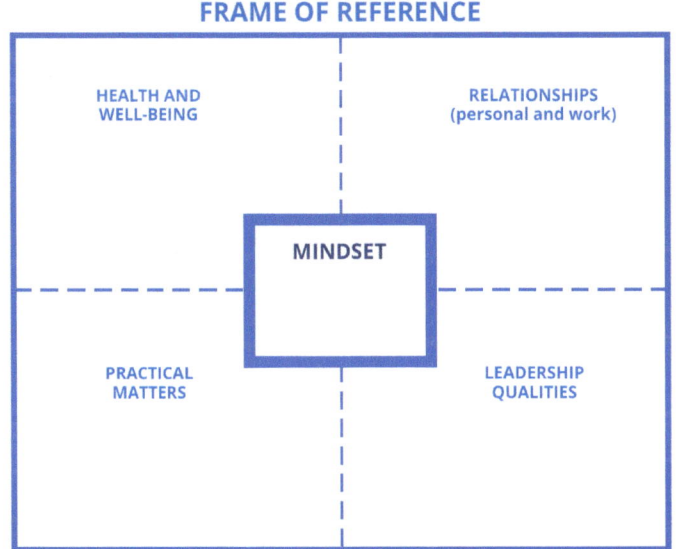

SELF-ANALYSIS – SUMMARY

First, thank yourself for taking time to pause and reflect.

Think about:

What have you learned about your leadership, pressures, stress reactions, and coping habits?

Which ones do you want to keep and cherish?

What would you like to change?

Summarise what you have learned.

CHAPTER 3

CHERISHING AND REFINING MY LEADERSHIP

Thank you for taking time to pause and reflect. Let's now explore what you would like to do next.

First, think about how prepared you are to challenge yourself. And how ready you are to explore the unknown and uncomfortable.

If you want to focus on adapting and shifting your current leadership qualities and behaviours, then finish your exploration here. If you want to explore in more depth, then please look at the next section before creating a plan for change.

Either path is acceptable. We all have moments when we want to resolve hidden issues to grow and learn, and times when we just want to lightly refine who we are.

Here are some suggestions for you to consider.

Quality	Suggestions
Personal assets	
Sacrifice and simplicity	What can you do to simplify your leadership practices and life? Perhaps decrease your reliance on material goods. Reflect on how you decide and then simplify the process.
Integrity, kindness, and concern for others	Why not start a practice of being or saying something that is kind, has integrity, and shows concern for others meaningfully? Pause, at least once a day, to see how kind you have been, where you have shown integrity, and whether you have compromised.
Peace for yourself and others	Create space and time, both physically and in your mind, so that you can build in more peace.
For people	Think about how you can expand and show your intention to be present for and aware of concern for others. Perhaps, make sure that your decisions benefit more than yourself or the organisation. How well do you look after the people for whom you are responsible?
Looking after personal mental health, physical health, and well-being	Make sure that you have a proper physical health check, at least annually. Think about how you maintain your mental health and well-being. What else do you need? Build on this by looking at your coping strategies.

	Learn about and manage uncertainties and pressure at work and in life.
	If you have a history of mental health issues, then please ensure that you have in place all the adjustments you need. This includes space for retreat and recovery if needed.
	Honour and embrace your diverse identities and neurological differences to find synergy in your life.
Accepting and recognising the role and influence of the past and present (resolved and unresolved)	Take a few moments to acknowledge your past (events and people). What memories feed you? Which ones do you need to let go of? Perhaps have a closure ceremony for them.
	Find ways of celebrating your past, anniversaries, and significant people in your life.
Work qualities	
Understanding, fairness, and equanimity	Learn about how to remain open in your thinking and decision-making. Learn about reflective practices and stoicism. Talk to a philosopher or someone from a very different world to yours. For example, an artist, and find out how they understand and judge.
	Talk to staff on how to promote collective accountability- praising the positive and addressing toxicity.
Living values and purpose	List them. Think about when you have lived up to them and when you have compromised. Work out how you will cope with compromise, e.g., make a reparation, forgive yourself, pray. How will you encourage yourself to take the higher ground next time?

Admitting fault with humility	No-one is perfect. We are all fallible. It is when we admit fault and when we let others see our frailty that we grow. What can you say the next time you make a mistake, so that you and everyone involved can learn openly?
Knowing how to communicate and interact	Actors know about the many ways of communicating, sensing, and interacting with others. Ask for feedback from significant people about your communication style. Work to improve it by having some sessions with an actor.
Understanding complexity	We often download and repeat what we have done, especially when faced with a new situation. Learn from eminent artists and work out how to free your thinking so that you allow yourself to go into "free fall" when facing a complex situation. Practise breathing, relaxing, and emptying your mind to enable this state.
Knowing the difference between leadership and governance	What is the difference between governing and leading? How is it enacted in your world? Governors are responsible for oversight and general guidance. Leaders focus on enabling the organisation to set and enact the vision. At senior levels, we can believe we are expert in many things. While we aren't novices, we have limits to our expertise, knowledge, and role. Understand this with other leaders and governors so that you can all work to activate the mission.

Dealing with crises	Successful crisis management is difficult. You need a balance of being calm; working from principles, not past examples; and knowing when to be democratic and when to be autocratic. The best way to learn is to talk to experienced others, e.g., those in emergency services. Practise, practise, alongside gaining theoretical knowledge.
Thinking strategically	To do this, you need to understand the core principles and concepts of running an organisation. Work out whether you are good at this or if you prefer the operational. Speak to philosophers and theoreticians to ask how to improve your skills. This is very important in this world of risk aversion, with so many protocols and risk management systems. Especially because these can lead to people not getting the job done because they focus on fulfilling the protocol.
Creating a work environment that facilitates well-being	Many will profess to know what is needed to create a work environment that promotes well-being. Some accommodations may be required. Typical interventions involve promoting self-care and mental health awareness and providing employees and managers with access to mental health specialists. Organisational interventions should include fair HR policies, decent salaries, and respectful work environments.

	Talk to colleagues and staff themselves to review what is in place and what needs to be enhanced. Don't just implant something from another organisation.
Treating others with dignity and respect	Consider how you treat others. How do other people show dignity and respect? Think about how you can change what you say and do to enhance dignity and respect. If you do this, then others will follow. This will have a greater impact than insisting on a code of practice.
Paying attention to community and world responsibilities	We can all be insular and selfish, even today when there is so much global concern and worry about conflict, global warming, and the lack of sustainability. Look at your leadership and your organisation. What actions can you take to ensure a legacy for the community and the world beyond ESG? Change your profit model?

Our coping strategies maintain us in our role in the world. Some of them are very important and valuable to us. These are the ones that we may find it hard to change.

It is worth recognising this.

And consider what will help you keep your cherished habits and strategies. They are vital to you.

Remember how you change, and how ready you are for this shift. Take some moments to reflect on this. If you are not ready for action, then allocate time for pause and reflection to consider how you could motivate yourself for change. Or do you need to wait until you are ready?

We have already made some suggestions for your leadership qualities. Here are some others.

FRAME OF REFERENCE

HELPFUL COPING

HEALTH AND WELL-BEING
Active self-care plan
Accepting the past
Balance
Maintain mental health and physical health
Beliefs and faith

RELATIONSHIPS (personal and work)
Personal relationships maintained well
Good quality support is available throughout

MINDSET
Good self-respect,
Values/Purpose honoured,
History respected

PRACTICAL MATTERS
Managing finances
Decent place to live
Reasonable transport
Enjoyable recreation

LEADERSHIP QUALITIES
Personal assets and work qualities utilised fully and honourably

HEALTH AND WELL-BEING

There are so many well-being interventions and advice available. We could just give you a list from which to choose. Let's have a different approach. Here are the key areas. Look at each one, think about what will benefit you and how you can achieve that outcome. Choose activities that are available and ones that you can fit into your daily life.

Manage your pressures and stress reactions – the aim here is to find ways of incorporating them and reducing adverse stress reactions. Start by creating a mindset/role that respects you and your self-esteem. You can do this by practising slow breathing and clearing your mind. Building a new mindset/role can start by creating a sentence that describes the new you. Then think about the behaviours that you would use. Imagine yourself using these actions. Practice these until they become second nature.

Key areas to build on include physical actions, healthy living (eating and consuming fluids, sleep). Look at your relationships so they are supportive and not destructive. If they are not helpful, then think about what you can do to adjust those relationships. If you cannot alter those relationships, think about what you can do to enhance your self-care.

Your work habits can help or hinder your self-care. Think about how efficient they are. How much pause and reflection are built in? How do you ensure that you stay focussed on your central responsibilities? What changes do you need to make to stay mission-focussed?

Maintaining your mental health and physical health is vital. Keep what you need and add to those actions. Build in interventions to help you if your health deteriorates – support from trusted people or healthcare professionals.

For some of us, our beliefs and faith are front and centre in our lives. If this is true for you, then ensure that they give you the succour you need. How can you maintain your practices and rituals?

An excellent outcome for practical matters is to ensure that they benefit your life rather than hinder it. Have good financial management and live somewhere that is conducive to your lifestyle. Your transportation should be facilitative. Your recreational habits ought to be helpful and fun.

SELF-ANALYSIS – MY PLAN

My new frame of reference: mindset/role and associated behaviours and actions.

Behaviours I want to cherish.

Behaviours I want to change.

Behaviours I want to let go of.

My action plan (describe with timeframes, resource requirements, and reminders).

SECTION TWO

LEARNING ABOUT AND LIVING WITH THE UNDERLYING AND UNRESOLVED

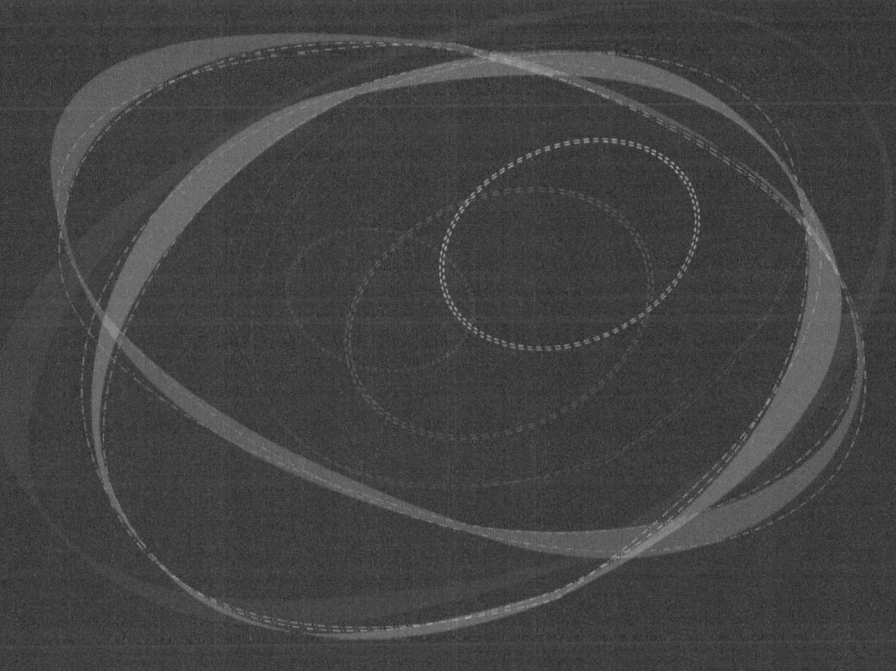

INTRODUCTION

Globally, we lurch from one example of poor, unethical behaviour and acts to another. All committed by leaders who should know better. Without respite.

Senior people who, despite being admonished for acts that depict a lack of ethics and integrity, prosper and carry on. Critics of these behaviours are seen as mere complainers. And there is a reluctance to accept the truth of such immoral behaviour.

What effect does this have on the rest of us? It almost anaesthetises us to awfulness, allowing us to cope and manage. But these behaviours impact our cognitive systems (thinking, memory, decision making) and likely affect our frame of reference for life. They may lead to us to be more inclined to be unethical.

Even if we have had a wonderful upbringing and life, there may well be some parts that we have not made peace with or are just downright ignoring. Omitting these factors may have helped us cope and grow as leaders, but there are often aftereffects. For instance, our parents taught us to be competitive with our siblings and we learned to suppress feelings of jealousy. But this may lead to us taking a dislike to a subordinate who we perceive as more competent.

Some of us have faced challenges and overcome them by reflecting, growing, and sometimes getting professional help. *Rogin had a very deprived upbringing and a limited education, so the only job they could get was as a waiter. But they knew they wanted more. Rogin left their home country, moved, and studied part-time to become an engineer. They became successful but had significant problems with building and keeping relationships. They lacked the knowledge of how to care for others and receive support. And they didn't feel they needed to bother. Until this was impeding their plans to build a big engineering practice. They realised that creating a good physical work environment was useless without caring for staff.*

Others will keep the unresolved front and centre, even without recognising it. *They brought Fredo into an organisation, as there were significant financial problems. The founder, William, had lost interest and people were taking advantage. Fredo's upbringing encouraged the use of underhand methods to steal people's ideas and thoughts and claim credit for them. Fredo re-built the organisation and its reputation. Leaders soon realised Fredo had a habit of stealing other people's work and ideas. The organisation asked Fredo to leave. They moved on to another company and were let go because the same problems had occurred. Fredo took no responsibility for their actions. As they said, 'it's only business.'*

So, we all have resolved and unresolved parts of us, as individuals and as leaders. These need not impede us too much, but we must make sure that they do not contribute to our own toxicity or that of the organisation. If we keep the unhelpful in our lives, then we are likely to replicate and promote it at work. For example, deliberate wilful ignorance allows us to be selfish even though it prevents us being altruistic. Such behaviours are facilitated if we see others doing the same.

The absolute failure to tackle organisational toxicity is, we argue, because of our permissiveness in letting it continue. This includes our reluctance to face our own unresolved parts that can lead to poor behaviour.

This section provides you with an opportunity to explore, safely, the resolved and unresolved. Make sure that you are ready and prepared to go on this journey of self-exploration. If you are not, then please wait until it is the right time for you.

This section is not about "cleansing yourself" but about learning to recognise your humanity and fallibility. A chance to explore how you live with yourself and your leadership. How you cope with resolved and unresolved parts of yourself.

If you give yourself this permission to explore and rebalance your golden and shadow aspects, AMAZING things could happen as you release more of your inner creativity and energy.

ABOVE AND BELOW THE SURFACE

Our history shapes who we are. It explains who we are, but it should never be an excuse. Let's start by exploring your history.

Here are some exercises for you to consider. You don't have to try each one. You can always mix and match the questions. The important thing is to choose something that will allow you to learn and explore your unknown, unresolved parts.

A. MEMORIES AND VOLCANOES

Look around you. What do you have that reminds you of your past? Photographs, songs, a cushion, furniture? Gather these items and others that enable you to recall your history.

Choose a time and place for reminiscing. Have your items around you. Perhaps invite a trusted one as your companion.

Let the memories return, one by one. Focus, first, on the helpful and happy ones. Pause and reflect with each one. Make a note of what has come back.

Remember to be careful if the memories have negative connotations. Only recall them if you feel safe enough. If they are sad or traumatic, then you don't need to relive every single minute, but only consider what the overall feeling was and what you learned.

What effect do these memories have on your current life and leadership? What has been resolved and what has not?

At the end of this, find a way of saying thank you to each memory and then either keep them or find a way of saying goodbye to them. For example, write key parts of the memory on a piece of paper and then destroy it.

(You can do the exercise above for each decade of your life.) Now please answer these questions.

How would you describe your current character? Thinking back to when you first had a sense of your character, what has changed?

Describe all the behaviours you use to lead. What is their history? What maintains them?

How has your past influenced who you have in your life?

How do the people in your life reinforce your helpful leadership? Who detracts from it?

What maintains your current self-esteem and respect? How constant is it?

What are the resolved and unresolved issues in your life? These are the volcanoes, and we have different types.

Volcanoes come in various sizes and states, some are dormant, some are active, and some just simmer. Sometimes volcanoes erupt on their own or get triggered by something within us or the world. The impact of a volcano can vary depending on the trigger, us, and the circumstances in which we find ourselves.

Think back to last year. What difficult and awkward moments did you have? How did you cope in the moment and afterwards? How were these moments triggered and by what? What was the link to your past and unresolved matters?

What types of volcanoes do you have in your life?

- ❐ Dormant and resolved
- ❐ Minor, unresolved, and unlikely to erupt
- ❐ Minor and sometimes erupting
- ❐ Major and often erupting
- ❐ Major, kept at bay, and unlikely to erupt
- ❐ Another type

What triggers them?

- ❐ Work
- ❐ A person
- ❐ Stress

- ☐ Sudden and unexpected event
- ☐ Anxiety
- ☐ Worry, e.g., about the climate
- ☐ Something else

How do the volcanoes affect your leadership behaviours?

Suki realized she had one item in her apartment that reminded her of her family history – a painting that had belonged to her father. The other ornaments were linked to her work, e.g., items bought in the countries where she had worked. She did not have any photos on display.

Doing the exercise helped her realise she had many volcanoes that were dormant, some resolved, but the majority were not. She acknowledged she had to look at them and find a way of making peace with her past.

B. PROTECTIVE AND RISK FACTORS

We each have a range of factors that are protective and allow us to live our lives, e.g., an interesting job. We also have risk factors, e.g., financial problems or a difficult relationship with a partner. It is worth stopping and identifying the ones that apply to you.

What are your current protective factors? What are your risk factors?

Make a note of what you have learned.

C. MY LIFE

Our lives revolve around self-confidence, relationships, mental and physical health, morals, and purpose. These are in our present and influence our behaviours and thoughts. Our history has informed these qualities. Both the past and present impact our future. Please find a quiet time and place and think about these areas, both the helpful and the unhelpful. Note down any reflections, then answer the questions below.

What were the key events in your history? Who were the significant people? How do these influence you today? Whose "voice" stays with you?

How much self-confidence, self-esteem, and respect do you have?

How much strength and courage do you have?

Far too much ....Not enough

What traumatic or difficult events happened to you? How do they have an impact today?

What strategies do you use to cope? You can choose more than one.

- ❒ Am realistic and have resolved most issues
- ❒ Deny what happened
- ❒ Dismiss and ignore what occurred
- ❒ Distract myself by focusing on other issues
- ❒ Am easily triggered back to what happened

- ☐ Suddenly get stuck or flummoxed when a trigger appears
- ☐ Have good coping strategies to cope with the influence of what happened
- ☐ Numbing and suppressing
- ☐ Self-sabotage

Relationships

Who is in your life? Who is supportive of you and who is not?

Emotional regulation

Which emotions do you allow in your life? Where, in your body, do you feel them? How good are you at managing and regulating them?

Very poor regulation .... Very good regulation

Morals and purpose

What are your morals and purpose? How much do you use them in your daily life?

Very limited impact .... Adhere to them rigidly

Mental health

How much does your mental health affect your daily life? How well do you look after yourself?

Physical health

How much does your physical health affect your daily life? How well do you look after your physical health?

The external world

How much does the external world influence you? Where you live and work, the impact of climate change, your community, news, and the media, etc? How important are material goods to you?

Based on all your answers, how would you describe yourself? What is your frame of reference (mindset and role (aka identity))?

I am

What does your statement say about your approach to decency? What would your close friends, partner, and family say about your statement?

Looking back on his life, Alan realised that there was much he could be grateful for. A loving family adopted him and helped him grow up. They encouraged him to be all he wanted to be, a successful academic and leader. Colleagues respected his work and approach as a leader.

However, he suppressed thoughts of his birth parents. Only when he heard that his birth sister was looking for him did he realise how much being adopted had influenced his frame of reference (mindset and role).

SUMMARY

Consider your known and unknown leadership style and behaviours, both resolved and unresolved. Describe them and identify what the underlying components may be and what their impact and influence are.

What have you learned?

Pause and think about your frame of reference (mindset and role). Imagine you have a blank canvas in front of you. What is the image that best describes all your facets, the golden and the shadow? For example, a mask with half a smile and one eye closed. Or a flowering plant that is growing despite the shade and stony ground.

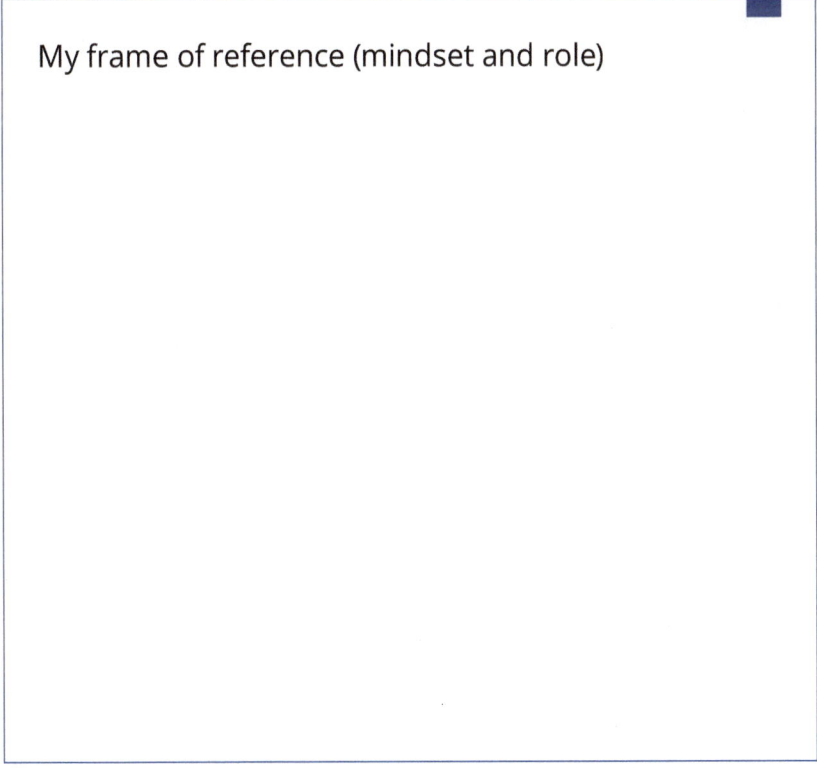

My frame of reference (mindset and role)

REBUILDING YOUR FRAME OF REFERENCE

To do this, it is important to recognize and name the issues that help and hinder your frame of reference and its development.

Please read through the following and identify what applies to you. Make a note of these.

We use Freud's defense mechanisms to explain, partly, how we can hinder ourselves.

WHAT CAN GET IN THE WAY?

The perfect me

Being golden includes compassion, kindness, and thoughtfulness. Shadow refers to not just malicious acts such as bullying and harassment but also lesser behaviours such as doing something that is not good for you. We each have these elements and we should be mindful of the continuum between golden and shadow. We can explore our golden and shadow sides, but we don't always find it easy. And sometimes, if we are not feeling strong enough, we will by-pass the reflection for the moment.

Why? We have built up an image of ourselves and we think it is almost perfect. Often, we have two realities: the one that we have created and the actual one. For example, saying that you are on a diet, except on Fridays when you eat whatever you want. All the food consumed that day counteracts your adherence to the diet on the other six days. You gain weight but pretend you haven't, even though you must buy bigger clothes.

So, we don't like it when there are issues that are contrary to our golden side and overall life balance. We can be brilliant at denying the obvious. For example, ignoring intuition when deciding to like someone. And then being surprised when that person harms us.

We need to work on what is shadow and unhelpful in us that leads us to ignore our positive intuition. What is stopping us and how can we change, given this is not a new behaviour?

We need to mature so that we become more willing to look at both our unhelpful shadow side and helpful golden aspects. This requires courage and a willingness to explore ourselves, some of which may be uncomfortable. Perhaps identify what triggers us into feeding our shadow side rather than the golden? For example, working from the shadow side can occur when self-esteem is low, and we want to reinforce that. So, what else can we do to feed our self-esteem rather than diminish it?

Perhaps imagine a conversation between the helpful parts of our self-esteem and the unhelpful aspects. What support could the helpful parts give to the unhelpful aspects, so that they diminish? And what new mindset do we need? We could plan a ceremony to say goodbye and thank you to the unhelpful parts?

Amazing things could happen if we took the time to reflect on ourselves as individuals and organisations in society. Isn't this the fundamental way in which we can progress and say enough to negativity? Isn't this our obligation because there is so much negativity that we permit – tacitly and overtly?

Ignoring personal care and well-being

Being a leader can feel like running on a circular treadmill while being pushed in several directions. So, it's difficult to stay centred and make sure you look after yourself. Especially if you have a history of problems and self-esteem that can fluctuate. Or if you have a lot of personal issues you ignore.

This is when people revert to the less helpful behaviours, such as using addictive substances, e.g., alcohol. Or ignoring the warning signs that your mental health or physical health requires attention.

It is vital to take time for proper selfishness and to build and maintain a personal self-care plan for well-being.

Not again

We have so much data that streams into our life. It is hard to stop and look at the field of information and associated emotions without feeling overwhelmed. Keeping looking, even though we know it does not help, can become addictive.

And some of this information is about people and events that have led to a lot of unethical behaviour that inevitably hurts and damages. This may adversely influence us if we are not careful.

How can we develop a different approach? Think of what is core to your integrity and values. How have you lived by or challenged these qualities in the past year? By whom (include yourself) and by what (for example, world events)? What did or should you have ignored?

Think of how intact your integrity and values are. What do you need to bring them more into shape so that you can feel less overwhelmed and more centred? Perhaps start with judging what the data is and then decide to listen or dismiss it.

Have a higher aspiration and keep that in mind. Martina McBride's song "Broken Wing" is about a woman who leaves an abusive relationship. She did this by "keeping an eye on the sky".

What happens around us and in us can have a helpful or unhelpful influence. It is in our gift to decide what influences us and we can choose how we will respond and live by our values.

Let's support each other to remind ourselves of our higher aspirations so that we can be the example of the improvement that we are looking for.

Self-sabotage

Why do we do this? We know it is not helpful, not healthy. But sometimes we go down that path of hurt.

Each of us possesses helpful and unhelpful ways to respond to the world. We learn these from others or even watching TV. The actions and thoughts we choose to include in our repertoire and use are a personal choice.

Our use of healthy or destructive habits depends on our self-respect and self-esteem. If we are confident, even in the moment, then we are unlikely to self-sabotage. If we have low self-esteem, then we may use behaviours that make things worse: missing a reasonable deadline knowing that your boss will shout at you.

A leader says: "if you go ahead with this, there will be heavy consequences". If your self-respect is low, you may think that it is normal to say such things and not "see" the threat. And then you don't carry out the action.

Sometimes we can be so used to hurt that we seek to keep it in our lives even when there is great personal risk, e.g., where there is a history of violence.

To let go of the tendency to self-sabotage, you must decide to shift to a more helpful view of yourself. Why have you self-sabotaged and how? Does it allow you to reinforce your low self-worth? Or do you see it as an emotional release or a way of keeping safe? Keep asking why, why, until the answer emerges.

Then look at the habits you use to self-hurt. What else could you adopt that is more helpful? Choose ones that are helpful, not hurtful. If you are not sure, check with a trusted person. Plan ways of introducing the new habits into your life in a measured way. Plan for those triggers and moments when you may relapse. Perhaps, keep a coded note (phone/computer or on a Post-it on your fridge) to remind you to be more positive. For example, you could write STSS. SAFE. (Stop the Self Sabotage. You are SAFE.) Look at this regularly, taking time to pause and reflect.

Praise yourself when you have chosen a healthier action than self-sabotage. Pause and learn from those moments when you relapse.

Create an image of the healthier you. Imagine being that person. How do you feel? What do you do and say that is different? How can you adopt these practices?

If you are not ready to stop the self-sabotage, then please make sure you and others are safe. Even if you are in a toxic environment that exacerbates your self-hurt habits. Consider seeking professional mental health help.

We all can self-sabotage. And we can also learn to leave this tendency in our past where it belongs.

Denial

Perhaps the journey from denial begins when we accept our humanity and fallibility. All our frailties, our human condition. We will appreciate learning and that accepting errors is part of this. If learning becomes our goal, there is no shame in errors. They are important and a necessary part of our process to learn about ourselves and life.

If we do this, we will embrace our limitations as part of life, something to be expected because we are only human. Then we will not need to hide from ourselves and others.

Many times, we face life realistically, unless it is too hard. Or when we don't want to accept what is in front of us.

In 2023, Dominic Raab, the ex-deputy prime minister of the UK, resigned after an inquiry confirmed two serious claims against him. At no point did he admit fault but wrote of the "two adverse findings", almost as though they were anomalies. He said he was sorry for causing unintended stress but then followed up that statement saying that his actions were what the public expected of a minister.

Sometimes it takes time to admit a fault. Martin Rowson created a cartoon, linked to Richard Sharp's resignation as chair of the BBC, which had strong antisemitic features. The Guardian published and then withdrew this in 2023. Martin Rowson apologised but it took him time to do so fully. He initially apologized with a "mea culpa". Later, he suggested that any offense was up to the interpretation of the viewer, rather than the cartoonist's intention.

We are all capable of such defensiveness. Denying allows us to ignore reality and our faults, especially the uncomfortable ones: when we are told about our own toxic behaviours or when someone gives us feedback that we don't want to listen to because it highlights a part of ourselves that we have not owned. For example, going for a long and arduous hike just after the doctor has instructed you to take it easy.

Facing the truth can be too much and so we protect ourselves. We hide from the awfulness of the situation. Knowing that your work situation is toxic and yet you stay for financial reasons. Sometimes, we can refuse to "see" a partner for who they are because we love them and want to give them one more chance.

The journey from denial begins with being willing to face reality. And that can take time. First, recognise that change is necessary and let the acceptance happen in a way that suits you, ensuring that nobody gets hurt.

Helping someone through their denial will depend on how close you are to them. And if they can face reality. Learn how they are dealing with the situation and how much they want to face reality. Sometimes the job is to comfort silently rather than telling them they need to see the reality for what it is.

Every person's journey to healing is individual and should be their own. Not what we think they should do.

Impunity

When we see many around us doing what they want and getting away with it, what happens to us? For some of us, we note this and then carry on being decent. Others see it as permission to behave as they want and not as they should.

We have too much of this in our world. Global leaders who feel they can do what they want. Not fulfilling their duties to serve the populations who elected them, or to society. National and local leaders who promote themselves and their own selfishness.

Regardless, we can choose how we want to live. With impunity or with decency and consideration of others. We are more likely to live within the boundaries of our morals and purpose when we remember we are part of and responsible for a greater whole.

Inner core

Busy is often part of who we are. And we have a lot to do at work. Sometimes, when we are expected to be creative, we cannot meet those expectations. We become complacent and repeat what we or someone else has done. Because we are tired or afraid to release our creativity.

If you watch or learn about eminent artists, they will show you that getting in touch with the inner core is essential to creativity. This can mean you don't know what you will produce. Sir Terry Frost, an abstract artist, said that he never thought about painting when he was creating. When he realised he was painting, then he stopped being imaginative.

Watching a singer during a brilliant performance, you see they are lost in singing. See Elvis in the '68 Comeback Special in the section where he is on a square stage with just his band. You will observe those moments when he really sang the song as opposed to singing by rote.

See Lizz Wright singing. She closes her eyes as she moves into the song. Have a look at videos of B. B. King in concert. Often, he would close his eyes while playing.

What can we do to get in touch with our inner core and work more from that? First, we need a conducive operating environment that provides the permissions. Second, we need to be relaxed and trust ourselves more to let go. Then just give the green light to "empty" our minds and wait. Why not try?

Opening our senses

When an organisation discovers and addresses unhelpful behaviour, preventing its recurrence is often rare. What we need is to ensure that all affected have and receive mental health support. We need to recognize and respect survivors and ensure justice for all. There also needs to be structural and operational policy change, backed up by behavioural and cultural change. Recent events highlight the importance of these interventions.

The genuine sadness is that we, as organisations, lurch from one toxic incident to another. Be it bullying, harassment, or unwanted sexual behaviour. We don't learn and therefore, by default, allow innocent people to suffer. I wonder what it will take for us to behave differently and be willing to say: "this is no longer acceptable. Let's stop this".

What can we do to not only open our senses but also then act? Firstly, realise that the organisational culture may have slipped into somehow normalising these behaviours. Secondly, recognise how you respond when the awful happens. Do you acknowledge it, deny it, or ignore it? I often downplay traumatic situations because of my experience in conflict zones. Knowing this, I make sure that I am responding and with sensitivity.

Then pause, breathe, and assess the situation to make sure you are on point. Check with a colleague as it is difficult to be emotionless.

Work out the politics and identify the best way to address the situation. Then find your courage from somewhere to do something concrete. Mine, I've learned, comes from a sense of injustice and knowing that I have a responsibility to work for fairness, without arrogance.

Always keep going and trying to address the problem until there is a good enough resolution for all. Throughout, ensure that you are looking after yourself so that you can be as objective as possible. Make sure, when you can, that you allow your emotions space and time.

Let's try. For those affected, for us, and our communities.

Displacement

How we are treated or our insecurities can sometimes lead us to target others. Our manager shouts at us and so we yell at a subordinate.

Sometimes we discriminate against another because we can. At other times, we do it because of our insecurities or wanting to fit in. Being sarcastic to a particular team member because that is what everybody else does.

We could feel and act angrily because of something in our own life. But we could blame others and say that it is their fault that we show anger.

If we use these behaviours, then it is important to investigate our own reasons and stop the unhelpful actions. Because they cause a lot of psychological damage to the person and those around them.

Projection

We can project hidden facets that we consider unacceptable onto someone else: finding fault or disliking a staff member for making mistakes and appearing incompetent because you are afraid that your own level of ineptitude will somehow show.

Intellectualisation

Being someone who does not deal with emotions at any level can lead to you focussing on process rather than how people feel, especially in an emergency. While it is important not to be overwhelmed by emotions as a leader, some attention is needed to personal feelings – yours and others. Telling someone to refer to the well-being strategy when they say they are distressed is an example of intellectualisation.

Avoidance

Leaders are often very good at avoiding having to address the presence and use of toxic behaviours, either their own or someone else's. Leaders make excuses or move the person, or they tell colleagues to grin and bear it. This avoidance is partly why we still see so many toxic behaviours and cultures.

Some can also avoid dealing with difficult situations where there is a likelihood of conflict. Avoidance in any shape or form never helps. The issue will always re-emerge.

The first step to healing is to acknowledge that you avoid certain people and situations. Ask yourself why. Is it because of some unresolved part of your past? If so, what steps can you take to reconcile with the past? Regardless, think of how you can find the courage to stop avoiding and start rehearsing how you will deal with the issues.

Suppression

We all know how to suppress. And it can be helpful, especially in emergencies and crises. But long-term suppression, even if it helped you get through your childhood, means that you are delaying the inevitable. Stop and think about how much you suppress and when it is of use and when it is not.

Find ways of releasing your emotions at a safe time and place. Think about how you can suppress only when it is necessary.

WHAT HELPS TO HEAL?

Healing takes time and it involves a willingness to change and to appreciate all your wonderful qualities. Some of us will change but, if we haven't also adjusted our frame of reference (mindset, role, and behaviours), we may undo some of our achievements.

We must allow ourselves a chance to appreciate the helpful. And acknowledge that it will take time to find a new balance between the known and unknown parts of ourselves. It is a continuous journey of ups and downs.

Changing

It is important to take a few moments to understand how you change – both voluntarily and otherwise. If you are ready to change, what is the path you are likely to follow? If you are reluctant to change, what do you do?

Remember, it is often valid to resist change, especially in the early stages or if it has been imposed on you. It could be part of your path to change.

Taking small steps can be less frightening and, at the same, bring the change closer. Forcing people to change rarely works and can lead to lip service. For example, people saying that they will use a new protocol (which they did not want) but they just do what they have always done.

Here are some questions to consider:

What steps do you take to change if you are ready? What will you do if you are not ready?

What helps you shift from being reluctant to being ready?

Who/what will motivate you to maintain this shift?

How could you relapse or sabotage yourself?

We can sometimes choose to change and do so. But then we revert to old habits. This can be our pattern for change, so we do not alter for the better in the long term. How much is this your pattern?

Think about your current repertoire of habits (behaviours, thoughts, and emotions). Which ones help you maintain the current frame of reference and which ones interfere with your positivity? What is the future frame of reference that you want? What new habits do you need? How can you say goodbye to the old frame of reference?

Enabling voices

The journey to respect and decency continues even though there are those who want to keep their power, negativity, and privilege. Biases can exist in anyone, regardless of their diversity.

The #MeToo movement and #BlackLivesMatter have given strength and power to those who had to endure silently. Unfortunately, we still need to speak up and address inequality and downright discrimination.

Events in 2023 included the fact that organisations often poorly resourced or made token gestures towards initiatives for diverse staff.

When people have been used to being discriminatory, they are unlikely to believe that change is necessary. Because they could continue in the past, they feel they can carry on even when they are asked or required to change.

We must still speak up regardless of the bias in front of us. Even if we must do it discreetly for our own safety. Otherwise, all previous efforts will have been for nothing.

We need to address discrimination and negativity, so that we don't become bitter and angry, which will eat us up. Because of the emotional cost of speaking up, we must look after and support each other in this endeavour. This is worth so much to us and the generations to come.

We need to say that it still matters. It still matters. It still matters, regardless of how tiring it is to keep giving the same message that discrimination needs to stop and that we should work for inclusion.

"We who believe in freedom cannot rest until it comes." Ella Baker.

"Hatred is never appeased by hatred in this world; it is appeased by love. This is an eternal law." Dhammapada. The Buddha.

Hope with courage

Around us, we have leaders who seem intent on helping themselves, not serving the public as they should. We have individuals and groups following suit, operating for themselves and being amoral.

We have people in our lives who will speak of the greater good and then do something that is the exact opposite. And they will justify themselves.

This can put your head in a spin and make you forget your core values. What does doing the right thing mean? Does is it matter if I lie or take credit for someone else's idea? Aren't these minor issues compared to someone being given a massive contract because of who they know?

Yes, but it is a slippery path that we tread if we carry out small, unethical acts. Our sense of what is acceptable and responsible blurs, and we can move onto bigger acts.

Most of us remain on the ethical side of life. Sometimes we err but we will recognise this and put things right.

What helps us is to know what our boundaries are for life in all aspects: materially, socially, and psychologically. What is the bottom line in each area below which we will not go?

And to realise that even in today's muddled and confusing world, it is important to have hope in ourselves, to stay true to who we are. We also need to have hope that each of us, individually and collectively, can make a difference, even if it is small. We make this easier if we remember and use our strengths and courage.

What does hope mean to you?

How can you use your courage?

What can you do to bring hope to yourself, others, and the world?

Carrying out an act that requires courage can help you feel good. Especially the first time you act. You may feel awkward and unsettled because of the aftermath. It may take you some time to act with courage consistently.

Freeing the inner spirit

Freeing the inner spirit is an essential part of decent leadership. Both in ourselves and the people for whom we have responsibility. This is key learning for us as an employee and leader.

Enabling a person to express themselves in their work and tasks is crucial to avoid mediocrity. However, some jobs, like piloting a plane or managing a crisis, require stifling creativity for safety and security reasons.

Apart from these situations, when we allow the expression of inner spirit, it's stunning what can happen. Have a look at the video of Bruce Springsteen singing Better Days (InConcert: MTV Unplugged) with his band. Each musician and singer felt they could be themselves. In contrast, watch

Michael Bolton singing Love is a Wonderful Thing (Live). This is still a brilliant performance, but there is more structure within which the performers could express themselves.

Learning to facilitate this requires giving yourself the permission to allow your own inner spirit and difference to show. To move into what Otto Scharmer calls presencing. This is easier with more experience and knowing that you can trust people and yourself. And being ready for those moments when something goes wrong. Then you can help the person in a helpful and non-blaming way.

Part of being a leader is to know how to liberate the inner spirit of the person and when it is OK to show it at full force and when to tone it down. We also need to know when to step back and let the person outshine us, which is inevitable.

Each person has their own sense of spirit and will liberate it in their own way. And it is important to recognise, know, and facilitate their individuality.

It is these very qualities that we seem to have forgotten in our work, as we have become protocol driven and procedural, making us risk averse and likely to self-blame. We need some protocols, but not so many that they stifle people and their human spirit.

Strength of character

We are holistic, sometimes centred, as we navigate our way through the world. We can be strong, and, at other times, we are not our best self.

One thing that affects us is what happens. 2023 was a strange year that only, unfortunately, increased our worries. The rates of inflation, energy prices, global conflicts, work, and personal life issues. All this, on top of recovering from the Covid pandemic.

What can keep us strong is our sense of self-confidence, faith in ourselves, and the ability to cope with whatever appears – our strength of character. What are the five words that describe this quality? Perhaps, kindness, determination, integrity, care and sense of fun. Which ones apply to you? What else would the best person in your life say?

Think of an image that depicts your strength of character. Anticipate what could happen –both helpful and unhelpful. How could you use your strength to live through the next year? Which parts of you could get in the way and why? What is underneath this tendency to get in the way? How could you face and diminish these and build your strengths?

With this knowledge, imagine that you are walking through the year. Remember this journey. This may help you be ready. Perhaps keep the image of your strength of character in a place where you can look at it regularly.

Being open

"Having moved to live by the sea, it was disconcerting to see the frequent daily tidal changes. And how easily the wind can create powerful waves. It took some time to adjust to this. Then I realised that this is symbolic of life. How much it changes and shifts, especially now. This can make us feel uncertain and, sometimes, worried."

It is at these times that we need to look at our routines and habits and identify which ones are helping us and which are not. And to wonder if we are sticking to them because doing so provides familiarity and comfort.

List your uncertainties and worries. Which ones can you do something about, and which do you need to accept? Which of your habits and routines are helping you to cope with the uncertainties of today, e.g., good self-care? What needs to be strengthened and what needs to be let go?

Uncertainty and habits are part of life. Sometimes we need to let go and flow with the waves and be open to uncertainty. And perhaps, from that stance, explore the usefulness of our habits.

Doing this allows you to remain centred and true to your inner core and purpose. For example, the ability to be kind and decent towards yourself and others remains, regardless. Our circumstances can influence how we show these qualities but ought not to stop us.

Permission to look back

Give yourself space, time, and permission to face the past. The more we do it, the more we heal.

The past will always be with us. We will resolve some of it and be peaceful, and other parts will not be. Sometimes it can help to look back, even to incidents and experiences that you thought you had resolved. Every time you do that, you heal a little more.

Sogu had been in an abusive relationship, but they got the courage to leave. They moved to another city and got a job as a manager. Sogu's dedication and resilience led to a promotion and the discovery of a new partner. They were happy. One day, by chance, they met their old partner at an airport. The person spoke to them for fifteen minutes as they were on their way to catch a plane. Sogu was upset and shocked but handled the situation well. Afterwards, they realised they had grown and healed a lot more than they had realised. Sogu recognised that healing is a continual process.

> **Make a note of what you have learned.**
>
> What are your resolved aspects and associated behaviours? What is their impact on you and others?
>
> What are the unresolved aspects and associated behaviours? What is the impact on you and others?
>
> What is the balance between them? What happens when you are off balance? And how do you reinstate equanimity?

Based on the above, what is your new frame of reference (mindset, character, and behaviours)?

What is the description and image? Make sure this helps you with your volcanoes.

What are the associated behaviours, feelings, and thoughts?

How will you introduce them into your life?

How will you maintain them?

You can incorporate some of this into your self-care plan. Other parts may require you to make time to reflect and learn more about yourself. People can do this by themselves or with a good and trusted companion. And sometimes it will help to see a therapist. We sometimes need more help than we can give ourselves.

SECTION THREE

WELL-BEING FOR YOUR TEAM

INTRODUCTION

Leaders are cognisant of the need to look after their teams. They recognise that, when this happens, they end up with employees who feel respected and have dignity. This often leads to greater productivity.

Well-being, as we noted earlier, is now a massive industry and there are many experts and interventions. It would be so easy in this section to give you a list of actions to take to implement well-being or, at least, double-check what you have in place.

However, we argue current interventions are like ready-made recipes with huge larders. We haven't checked the ingredients, found what the diners want, or the state of the kitchen or even the larder. This may be why there can be a limited uptake of such interventions.

Here's an alternative approach.

Remember, it may be wise to ask an external professional to lead this work even if there are very good levels of trust in the organisation. Staff may feel more able to be open with an outside facilitator.

JOINING THE DOTS

Changing the organisation for the better is what many claim. Leaders implement interventions to enhance culture, employee experience, mental health, and inclusion. They work on HR procedures, talk of decreasing presenteeism, building psychologically safe environments, and so on. We don't join the dots.

What we don't do is tackle the underpinning problems. A lack of decency and respect, a failure to have good inclusion and well-being. And we ignore toxicity and the interlinkages between toxicity, the need for mental health and well-being and inclusion.

Toxicity presents itself in people's behaviours and cultures. These are the very things that impede a quest for inclusion, for belonging, and to ensure mental health and well-being.

What we should do in organisations is map all these interventions and look at their connections and linkages. And then look to see where we are committing resources and energy. What meaning do these have for the overall aim of equality, fairness, and well-being? It should be decent organisations, leadership, and cultures in which people can thrive.

How would you populate this diagram for your organisation and, perhaps, for your leadership? How can you join the dots? What is working and what needs to be done differently? Only by answering these questions can we deliver an environment that is coherent, fair, and inclusive. We'll explore this later.

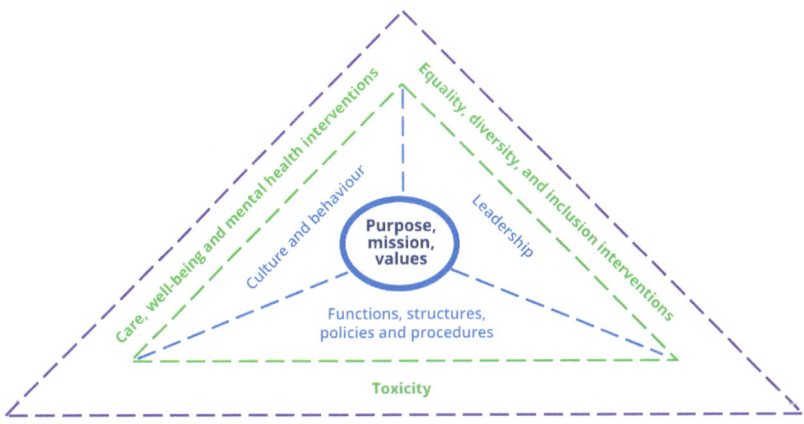

Global and community factors

FACTORS THAT IMPACT WELL-BEING

Leaders have a key role in ensuring and maintaining the well-being of their teams. This goes beyond having a well-being programme or an EAP department. Research reveals that, often, there is a very limited uptake of such initiatives to the extent that there is no significant impact on well-being in some organisations.

Part of the problem is that we rarely ask employees what they want. As we noted earlier, it's as though someone else has chosen the contents of their larder, selected recipes, and failed to ask if people are hungry and, if so, for what. Employers rarely ask employees what they want, even though they often have their own resources for well-being.

We need to ensure that we offer people opportunities to manage and look after their self-care and well-being. This leads to them becoming more productive and engaged.

What is also vital is the need to recognise and address those factors that impede well-being. And make sure that we tackle them alongside promoting well-being initiatives.

The leader's personal self-care and well-being

If the lead person does not look after themselves, then why should anyone else? Secondly, making sure of personal well-being means you are more likely to be respected and use helpful leadership behaviours. You are more apt to utilise behaviours that promote care and support while expecting staff to get the job done.

The team's history

A long-standing team, or one with a few people who have been there for some years, can maintain the culture, even if it has some shadow elements. If the culture is well-established or some have a lot of power, then it may be difficult to bring about change and introduce healthier self and team care.

Honouring and recognising the role of history is a crucial first step to help the team own and want to introduce better well-being practices. These must be meaningful to them, as opposed to off-the-shelf products.

Appreciating what is helpful and what is holding the team back in terms of thoughts, feelings, and behaviours is part of growth. For example, how has the team coped with stress and pressure in the past? What helps now?

Addressing mistakes or not

All of us, even expert leaders, are fallible. Eventually, we will make a mistake, or our team will. This is inevitable. It's how we deal with the aftermath that will contribute to how willing people are to admit errors.

Leaders must provide atmospheres and cultures that are open and enable people to do their best. And admit to errors so that everybody can learn. This permissiveness contributes positively to well-being.

When people work in fear of making mistakes and being found out and blamed, then they are likely to hide their mistakes if they can. Hiding or ignoring errors does not work and can have massive consequences for the company's productivity and reputation.

Teams must believe that they are working in an environment that is conducive to admitting mistakes. The leader must publicly state that and then show that people can trust them to be supportive when there are errors. Just saying it is not enough.

Sufficient skills and training

It can be rare for a leader to have the requisite skills, knowledge, and training to do the job, even if they have been on a course. Leadership programmes often focus on teaching concepts and can fall short on the application of the same.

This lack may make a leader feel insecure and then they may protect themselves by distancing or being over-critical of someone in the team (peer or subordinate) who is more qualified.

They may want to keep the team on alert and so be unlikely to introduce anything that leads to the team learning something they don't know, or which allows the team to flourish.

Therefore, a leader should reflect on their own skills and talents and make sure that they are fulfilling their growth so they can then lead with equanimity.

And they should afford as many opportunities as possible for the team to grow and learn – both formally and informally.

Mattering and work culture

Ideally, all employees and leaders should feel that what they do matters and that it contributes to the overall purpose. Often, purpose remains as words on a page and people do not fully live by it. Leaders speak about purpose and forget the reality. But there is often compromise, and we must acknowledge this.

Otherwise, this can impede well-being and a positive caring culture in which people feel respected and that they matter.

Ensuring that the right physical environment and culture is present, socially valuable, and maintained is vital – a necessary commodity.

Inclusion

The converse of discrimination is inclusion. There has been some progress but there is much more to do as we strive to achieve an intersectional world where all are welcome.

People are more willing to declare their differences and, rightly, have expectations of being part of a team. Some team members will be welcoming but others may shun the person, sometimes subtly. Inclusion of intersectionality for well-being should be led by everybody present so that they create their own definition and work out how to enhance it.

It is also important to recognise that part of the journey towards inclusion will be uncomfortable. We need to examine ourselves, look at our biases, and work to be better members of society. If we don't, then we will perpetuate the stereotypes and other unhelpful actions that block inclusion.

We also need to do our utmost to welcome those who may require adjustments and accommodations to enable them to function at work. For example, people who are neurodiverse, e.g. have qualities of ADHD and autism, all deserve a chance to succeed as much as anybody else.

Discrimination

The most recent global research points out that discrimination abounds for most differences. Sadly, discrimination in the workplace is also common. For example, diverse groups are often over-qualified for their posts, and they experience regular discrimination, e.g., insults and devaluing jokes. These then negatively affect people's mental health and well-being.

As a leader, it is vital to examine your own approach to diversity. Both in terms of your attitudes and your behaviours. What are your own biases and preferences? How do you ensure they don't adversely affect your leadership? What is your sense of privilege? How do you make sure that you don't keep your privilege at other people's expense?

What do you do to encourage your team to be more comfortable and open about diversity and difference? What do you do to promote it?

Mental health

Mental health can vary from day to day. Some of us with mental health problems need to manage and cope while balancing work and a career.

For there to be staunch support for well-being, a leader must create, by example, openness when talking about emotional and mental health. Perhaps by sharing their own experiences or those of close family members (with permission). By creating spaces (physical and virtual) in which people can take time out. For example, having meetings in which staff can talk about the emotional impact of their work or providing space in supervision for personal issues if the staff members want.

The presence or absence of toxicity

Toxicity, however small, is present in every organisation. That is clear and there is substantial evidence to support this, both for individuals and organisations.

Those who work in such environments are likely to report poorer mental health and productivity is affected. Interestingly, in these environments, managers can consider that their employees' mental health is fine.

Leaders can actively promote an unhelpful environment by promoting those who support toxicity, ignoring those who are more capable, blocking diversity, and lacking compassion. Some leaders can tacitly promote negativity by pretending it does not exist.

When there is significant toxicity in an organisation, there is a massive fallout which is often not recognised. It can affect all reputations. Productivity is often low and not as much as expected.

Sickness and turnover rates are greater than expected. Higher levels of stress and anxiety occur, and so healthcare costs are likely to increase. Problems sleeping and unnecessary rumination can also occur. People can overfocus on unhelpful words and actions used to discriminate against them. There is fear, a sense of dread, and high alert – waiting for the next awfulness as well as lower cognitive skills, etc.

The mental health and well-being of those who experience discrimination and/or toxicity is adversely affected. They experience what Arline Geronimus terms "weathering", where individual mental and physical health systems are affected, much like the impact of the weather on the outside of a building.

A suite of well-being interventions often cannot adequately address these issues. People develop toxic resilience, which is the prioritisation of work over personal life. This may be because of compliance to avoid the awfulness.

All these reasons are exactly why a leader needs to address toxicity and discrimination alongside enhancing well-being and mental health. Not to do so means that you are simply trying to bandage a wound without addressing the underlying causes.

The first step is for a leader to look at themselves and examine their own approach to toxic behaviours. How have they contributed to such cultures? To what extent do they use these behaviours? How much courage have they had to tackle such behaviours and cultures sustainably?

How much do the company policies and procedures facilitate the need to tackle such behaviours? How are they used? Are they trusted?

What mechanisms are in place to ensure that prospective employees will not use these behaviours?

How supportive is the prevalent culture of inclusion and well-being?

What effect do current interventions for well-being and inclusion have?

Think about the external factors that could impact, e.g., the long-term effects of Covid, climate anxiety, worry over world events.

Analysis

1. Now, analyse the team and its environment using these continua.

Where would you locate the team? Where would they place themselves?

Caring leadership	Uncaring leadership
History helps	History blocks
Mistakes permitted	Mistakes hidden or ignored
Sufficient skills and development	Inadequate skills or growth
People matter	No-one cares
Discrimination rampant	Inclusion is present
Mental health acknowledged	Mental health ridiculed
Toxicity in abundance	Healthy culture

What have you learned?

2. Here is a diagram and table to guide your thinking. Look at each aspect of the organisation and complete the table. Do this with a cross-section of the organisation.

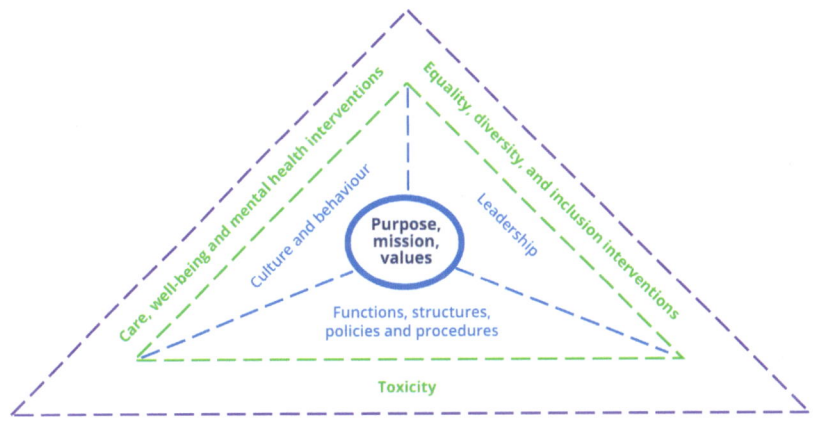

Global and community factors

Area	Impact on inclusion (helpful and unhelpful)	Impact on mental health and well-being (helpful and unhelpful)
Leader's behaviours		
Team behaviours		
Overall culture		
Functions		
Structures and policies and procedures		
Interventions for inclusion		
Interventions for well-being and mental health		
Toxicity		
External factors		

Think about each aspect (helpful and unhelpful) and consider which ones people want to keep and which ones they want to change or let go of.

INTERVENTIONS FOR TEAM WELL-BEING

Before we explore possible interventions, it is vital to ask what is the vision for well-being in your organisation? The employees should set this with leaders. All should collectively audit the helpful and unhelpful aspects of the organisation. This should identify issues that are well-being specific and those that need to be addressed, but are the responsibility of another department or leader, e.g., ensuring there is fair staff remuneration.

What type of employee and culture do you want? How can you enable this? How can you build from what people already do?

To what extent do you want collective accountability (praising the helpful and addressing the unhelpful) and what helps and what gets in the way?

Toxicity, weathering, discrimination – where are they present in your organisation?

How will you address them?

How will you promote a culture where people matter and their mental health is respected, regardless of how they are coping?

And so, what is your vision? What are the priority areas for action? How will you include staff in overseeing the interventions?

Look at what helps and hinders change. How willing is the team to recognise the need for change? What is the possibility of relapse or sabotage? How can you factor these issues into the change plan?

Interventions

Here are some interventions to consider.

Develop and implement a living code of practice for staff, specifying the desired behaviours and the actions to be taken if someone deviates from the agreed-upon norms. No gossip. Staying helpful. Help staff to be OK with setting limits.

Create a personal and corporate warning system for the re-emergence of toxicity and/or discrimination.

Look at existing team habits of behaviour and work. What needs to be cherished? What needs to change?

Research has shown that these factors are necessary for good team well-being and they could be considered.

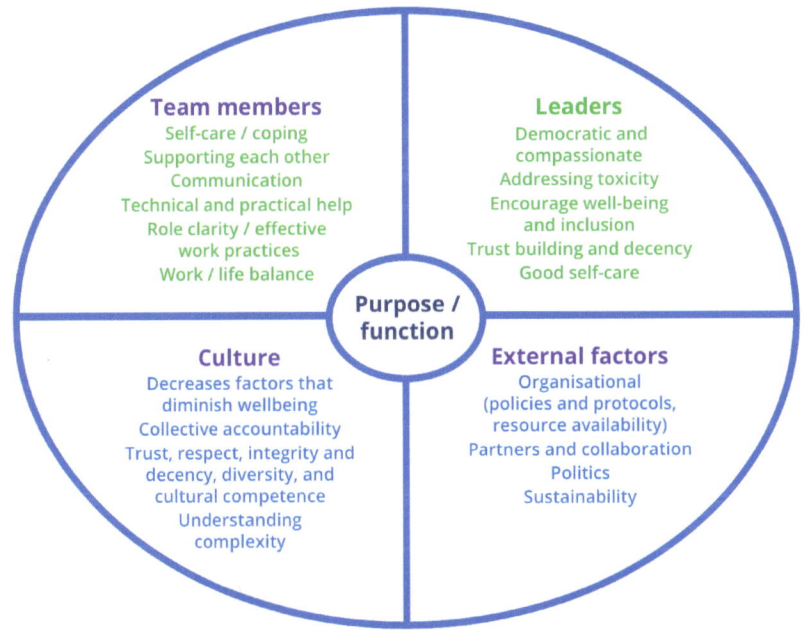

Why not use this model with the team? Ask them to add/change and adapt it to fit their needs. Then request that they use it to look at what is currently available. And what the gaps are. Work with the team to analyse the findings and develop a plan for change in three areas: individual actions, team actions, and leadership actions.

Make sure you create an environment for staff to self-reflect on their contribution (or not) to toxicity, mental health, and inclusion (theirs and other people's). And for all to continue learning and growing.

There is an interrelationship between the leader and the team. This will influence team well-being and the associated culture. Which is why leadership must look at their own approaches to well-being and the factors that impede it. Then address what or who gets in the way. Isn't that our moral obligation as leaders?

REFERENCES

American Psychological Association (2023). A nation grappling with psychological impacts of collective trauma. (https://www.apa.org/topics/stress) (https://www.apa.org/topics/mental-health) (https://www.apa.org/topics/trauma)

Bailey R, Pico J. Defense Mechanisms. [Updated 2023 May 22]. In: StatPearls [Internet]. Treasure Island (FL): StatPearls Publishing; 2023 Jan-. Available from: https://www.ncbi.nlm.nih.gov/books/NBK559106/

Bradshaw, E. L., Conigrave, J. H., Steward, B. A., Ferber, K. A., Parker, P. D., & Ryan, R. M. (2023). A meta-analysis of the dark side of the American dream: Evidence for the universal wellness costs of prioritizing extrinsic over intrinsic goals. *Journal of Personality and Social Psychology, 124*(4), 873–899. https://doi.org/10.1037/pspp0000431

Cambridge Dictionary (n.d). *Well-being*. https://dictionary.cambridge.org/dictionary/english/well-being

Ceniza-Levine, C. (2022, June 22). *5 ways to support the well-being of your team*. Forbes. https://www.forbes.com/sites/carolinecenizalevine/2022/06/22/5-ways-to-support-the-well-being-of-your-team/?sh=4925d39b2a2c

Centers for Disease Control and Prevention. (2018, October 31). *Well-being Concepts*. Centers for Disease Control and Prevention. https://www.cdc.gov/hrqol/wellbeing.htm

Cleveland Clinic. *Stress: Signs, symptoms, management & prevention*. (2021, January 28). https://my.clevelandclinic.org/health/articles/11874-stress

Eliatamby, A. (Editor) (2022). Healthy Leadership and Organisations: Beyond the Shadow Side. Shilka.

Eliatamby, A. (2023). The Decency Journey Pocketbooks. Shilka

Gallup. (2023a). *How to Prevent Employee Burnout*. Gallup.com. https://www.gallup.com/workplace/313160/preventing-and-dealing-with-employee-burnout.aspx

Gallup. (2023b, August 3). *What is employee wellbeing and why is it important?* Gallup.com. https://www.gallup.com/workplace/404105/importance-of-employee-wellbeing.aspx.aspx

Geronimus, A, (2023). Weathering: The Extraordinary Stress of Ordinary Life on the Body in an Unjust Society. Audible. (Alma Cuervo, Narrator). Hachette-UK

Hatfield, S., Fisher, J., & Silverglate, P. H. (2022, June 22). *The C-suite's role in well-being*. Deloitte Insights. https://www2.deloitte.com/us/en/insights/topics/leadership/employee-wellness-in-the-corporate-workplace.html

Hendy, E. (2023, January 18). *A clean break: The Wellness Industry isn't well, and people are finally waking up to it*. The Independent. https://www.independent.co.uk/life-style/wellness-scams-goop-pseudoscience-b2260871.html

International Classification of Diseases, Eleventh Revision (ICD-11), World Health Organization (WHO) 2019/2021 https://icd.who.int/browse11. Licensed under Creative Commons Attribution-NoDerivatives 3.0 IGO license (CC BY-ND 3.0 IGO).

Klebe, L. and Felfe, J. (2023). What difference does it make? A laboratory experiment on the effectiveness of health-oriented leadership working on-site compared to the digital working context. BMC Public Health (2023) 23:1035 https://doi.org/10.1186/s12889-023-15798-2

NHS Inform (2023). *What to do if you are struggling with stress.* (2023, January 4). https://www.nhsinform.scot/healthy-living/mental-wellbeing/stress/what-to-do-if-you-are-struggling-with-stress#:~:text=There%20is%20little%20you%20can,adopting%20good%20time%2Dmanagement%20techniques

Pendell, R. (2021, March 22). *Wellness vs. Wellbeing: What's the difference?* Gallup.com. https://www.gallup.com/workplace/340202/wellness-wellbeing-difference.aspx

Percy, S. (2022, November 9). *How can leaders help their teams to better manage stress?* Forbes. https://www.forbes.com/sites/sallypercy/2021/11/03/how-can-leaders-help-their-teams-to-better-manage-stress/?sh=7c7d9d9173a9

Raphael, R. (2023, July 26). *How Fake Science Sells Wellness.* The New York Times. https://www.nytimes.com/2023/07/26/well/live/wellness-products-false-claims.html

Rahula, W. (2006). Buddhist Cultural Centre, Sri Lanka.

Reynolds, E. Why do we engage in wilful ignorance? BPS https://www.bps.org.uk/research-digest/why-do-we-engage-wilful-ignorance 1/4

Ross, D.B. and Esposito J.A. (2023). Stress and its relationship to leadership and a healthy workplace culture. DOI: 10.4018/978-1-7998-0954-8.ch009

Rutledge, L. K. (2020, October 14). *Self-awareness as a key to self-care*. LinkedIn. https://www.linkedin.com/pulse/self-awareness-key-self-care-laurel-k-rutledge-mba-sphr-shrm-scp/

Wooll, M. (2021, April 8). *How to talk about well-being with your team*. BetterUp. https://www.betterup.com/blog/how-to-talk-about-well-being-with-your-team

World Health Organization. (2023, February 21). *Stress*. World Health Organization. https://www.who.int/news-room/questions-and-answers/item/stress#:~:text=Stress%20can%20be%20defined%20as,experiences%20stress%20to%20some%20degree

www.ingramcontent.com/pod-product-compliance
Lightning Source LLC
Chambersburg PA
CBHW041722070526
44585CB00001B/7